M.O.V.E. or Be Moved!

B. A. Ross

M.O.V.E. or Be Moved!

Edited by Rheadrea' Monet Walker

ISBN-10: 1977939945
ISBN-13: 978-1977939944
First Edition: October 2017

10 9 8 7 6 5 4 3 2 1

This Book is dedicated to my children; Julian, Dorien, Shallah, Londyn, Linda and Brookelyn. As I write these words I am also evaluating myself as a father and a leader. I will one day return to you all a better man. I hope you understand that the journey I have taken was one that I had to take alone. All that I've done, all that I've sacrificed I did it so that you all may have a better life, with me in it.

I LOVE EACH OF YOU THE SAME!

Table of Contents

"Our deepest fear is not that we are inadequate. Our deepest fear is that we are powerful beyond measure. It is our light, not our darkness, that most frightens us. Your playing small does not serve the world. There is nothing enlightening about shrinking yourself so that others around you won't feel insecure. We are all meant to shine as children do. We were born to manifest the power of God that is in us. It's not just in some of us; it is in all of us. And as we let our own light shine, we unconsciously give other people permission to do the same. As we are liberated from our own fear, our presence automatically liberates others."

-Marianne Williamson

Author of "A Return to Love"

INTRODUCTION

I sat in the living room before my mother came home from work enjoying my alone time, watching cartoons on T.V., before doing my homework. I figure I'd have all day to finish my tasks. Watching shows in the living room on that large floor model, as opposed to the 19" television in my bedroom, was a rare opportunity that needed to be taken advantage of. In my 11-year-old mind, that was more important than completing my homework. My mother arrived home from work asking, "any homework?"

"Yes." I replied.

"Is it done?" She asked.

"No." I answered with a slight mumble.

With understanding she says, "alright well let's get it done."

∞◊†∞◊†∞◊†∞◊†∞◊†∞

I saw homework as a controlling form of discipline. In my own mind I challenged the reason why we had to do work outside the working environment of school. Why did I have to come home and continue to do school work on my personal time?

What we failed to realize in our youth is that our parents already knew the importance of an education. Whether your parents graduated from high school or college or not at all, we all learned equally the importance of education. That's why our parents were hard on us; they knew how hard our lives could be without one. Our parents only want the best for us and they are willing to do whatever necessary to make sure that we reach our full potential. Some of us learn easy, others of course, learn the hard way. Those who were easy to coach learned the importance of education and were successful enough to complete high school. Those who were hard to coach may have not been so successful.

But what is success? You will find that every person will give you a different answer. Is there a permanent set of attributes that describes success? If success is different to each person, who is to say that there is only one road there?

Those "easy learners" make it to success in an easier fashion. Those who learn the hard way take a rockier road. However, success is available to us all. No matter how you define it, there is a way to achieve your idea of success.

∞◊†∞◊†∞◊†∞◊†∞◊†∞

My mom told me to turn off the television and complete my homework. I said 'okay,' but fell back into the trance that kept me glued to my seat watching my favorite show. When she returned, noticing there was no compliance on my part, she heftily blurted out "MOVE OR BE MOVED!"

Now, I'm sure many of you reading this book have heard the phrase, "so as it is in Heaven, so shall it be on Earth." Think about what that means to you. Don't think about what your pastor or minister at church may have told you. Ponder that phrase and find what it means to you, personally. I break this phrase down as follows (remember this is my *personal* take on it): To me, this phrase means that the same laws on Earth are the same ones followed in the Heavens. Notice, I used the word LAWS and not RULES. I don't mean laws as in the rules made by man and deemed as law. I am referring to the laws of life. Rules change. Rules can be broken. Laws remain the same and cannot be changed, revised, remixed or defied.

These Laws of Life can be discovered. Some of them defy laws of man. But, just because we just discovered it doesn't mean we invented it. For something to be discovered doesn't mean that you made it. It only means you found something that was already there that no one else had yet stumbled upon. (Dis-covered!) It was always there. You've just revealed to the masses what you've found. *What goes up MUST come down.* That is a law of life. No matter how you look at it, it will always remain the same and nothing can change that outside of the hand of God.

In this book, I'm going to share with you some laws of life that you MUST learn and abide by to be successful. There is no way around it, these are laws. You cannot bend the law. You must follow it to the letter or it will NOT work.

∞◊†∞◊†∞◊†∞◊†∞◊†∞◊†∞◊†∞◊†∞◊†∞

BEING CHOSEN

Matthew 22:14

"For many are called, but few are chosen"

Church became a big part of my life when I was eight years old. The first time I ever thought about committing suicide I was eight as well.

Later in life, I would learn that I suffered from depression and paranoia schizophrenia. Depression is a chemical imbalance of dopamine in your brain that causes you to have sad feelings. Paranoia schizophrenia is a condition where you convince yourself that certain things are going on that may not be true and you conduct yourself according to your own truth. The thing is; that truth is derived from a paranoia based on certain things in life you may have experienced.

The paranoia developed later in my life, after being kicked out and talked about by the very same people I thought loved me. I was homeless at the time and it happened so often that when people would allow me to stay with them I wouldn't go look for a job because I was too busy looking for and anticipating the boot. I convinced myself that no one wanted me around, even when they offered a place for me to stay. I conducted myself according to my own truth. Even to this day I fight my own thoughts about those around me. I've become introverted when I'm uncomfortable or unfamiliar with people around me. I tend to walk on egg shells as to not get in anyone's way or anger anyone. This paranoia has taken a normally outgoing, open, young man, and made him into a quiet, somewhat reserved, adult.

Being given up on was a huge part of my childhood. I never realized it until I was grown with kids of my own. As I reflect on my life, I realize that it was far from normal. My mother wasn't physically affectionate or even one to tell her kids 'I love you.' Don't get me wrong, my mom put clothes on my back, food on the table, and she worked hard to maintain a roof over our heads. She did only what she knew to do raising us. She did was she thought was right.

Whenever I think of my childhood I can never recall my mother being affectionate towards my brother Mark and me. In fact, I vividly remember her telling my brother and I that if she had to choose between us and her husband, our stepfather, that she would choose her husband. I was about nine or 10 years old. My mother was deeply into the church and I now realize that she said it because she felt it was the Christian thing to do. As an adult, I get it. I understand that her desire to please her God was stronger than her desire to please her children. However, there were a string of events that I didn't understand. The only way I began to understand my mother was by asking my aunts and uncles about her childhood. I never knew my grandfather but, I knew my grandmother well enough to know that my mom's lack of affection was due to how Mom-Mom raised her.

The other half of the reason my mother wasn't very affectionate with me is because I look so much like my father. My mother hated that man so much. He put her through so much with one child that she didn't want to bring another into an emotionally and physically abusive relationship. She didn't plan on giving birth to me. My father accused her of having another man's baby and out of desperation to prove him wrong; she gave birth to me.

This unplanned pregnancy launched my mom head-first into post-partum depression. Post-partum depression or "baby blues" is a condition some mothers experience after giving birth. It's characterized by mild depressive symptoms. My mom refused feeding me, playing with me or changing my diaper. These things didn't happen until my father or one of my aunts came by to visit.

∞◊†∞◊†∞◊†∞◊†∞◊†∞

As I grew older my depression grew worse. At age 12 in Jacksonville, FL I attended Landon Middle School. It was a three-story building with a castle-like design. My mother, brother, stepfather and I were preparing to go to Disney World for the weekend. My suicide attempt replaced my exciting weekend with a mandatory 72-hour watch after being Baker Acted by my school.

I said or did something inappropriate in class and was sent to the principal's office where they called my mother to inform her of my behavior. My mother asked Principal Sadler to pass me the phone. With the harshest tone I had ever heard from her, she said, 'when you get home, I'm gonna kill you.' I figured I wouldn't give her the satisfaction, so I walked back to my classroom on the third floor and tried to jump out the window.

I knew at age eight that I was different. Not the kind of different you can see in a person. I'm not even referring to my attempts or thoughts of suicide. No. I knew all my life that there was something lying dormant in my spirit that was just desperate to get out. I could feel it like there was another me, the real me, trapped behind all the negativity placed in my spirit throughout the years. The real me was buried under all this trash that was dumped into my spirit by my parents, my peers, ministers and therapists. The dual diagnosis of depression and paranoid schizophrenia was the biggest piece of trash ever stored into my being. No matter what was told to me, there was always a piece of me that knew I was destined to be great; 'change the world' great. No matter what happened in life there was always a distant voice in my mind or a tug at my spirit that said: 'You can't die now. You have work to do.'

I am head-strong. I will forever be that rebellious child sitting on the couch that day when my mother came home from work. I will forever carry that trait. I questioned the norm at every turn. I felt as if I could change the way life's laws worked. I questioned everything from religion to mathematics and what I found is that laws will never be changed. No matter how I tried to finesse my way around these things and take short cuts in life, I found there was just no way around life's laws.

∞◊†∞◊†∞◊†∞◊†∞◊†∞

Let's ponder Matthew, 22:14. "For many are called but, few are chosen." Once again, this is my personal understanding of this scripture. I believe we are all “called” to do something great on this earth. The evidence is in the very make up of who we are. I know I’m different. I know I was called to do something great! This thing that I am called to do is so great that God cannot afford for me NOT to step into my place on this earth. I am chosen. You are no different than me. If you are reading this book it means you are searching for answers. You are chosen by the Great Creator himself to carry out things on this earth that only you can accomplish. In the case that you do not complete your task there will be another person assigned to complete it. Whoever your replacement is; he or she isn’t you. They aren’t going to bring to the table what you would have brought. This leaves out those who needed to receive specifically what YOU have. They will NEVER be able to receive what you have for them. But the thing about being chosen by God, is that God knows what He’s doing. He’d never choose someone who would walk out on their calling. God would never choose a man or woman who would leave the job undone. No matter how hopeless it may seem sometimes, you are chosen. All roads lead to your purpose and you are destined to carry it out.

He chose me to help heal the broken because I was once broken. You must know what your audience is going through. When you know first-hand what people are dealing with, it amplifies the importance of service. To be an expert on any subject, you must first do research. To be an expert in life, you first must live.

There were times when things were so bad I thought that I couldn't possibly be made for what it is I've been called to do. I had to remind myself that everything experience is preparing me for something great. We all tend to get caught up in the vision and think that with one small quick fix, things will always be easy or that you will always be happy. That is a lie we consciously tell ourselves because we are so caught up with the end result.

There will be tough times. There will be pain. There will be times when you feel like you are in this world alone. Those are the times that build your character. You will question if God is truly with you, but if you are honest with yourself, you will see that He has never left you. You won't be passionate about what you are doing if you haven't paid a price for it. People tend to take better care of the possessions that they had to work hard to get. The things that are given to us, we take for granted. It's a natural human reaction. Nothing worth having comes without adversity. This is one of those life laws I spoke of previously. There's no way around the fire. You must go through it. The key is to not get stuck in it. These fires, these adversities, are tests administered by life's greatest teacher: experience. If you don't pass the test with 100%, you have to retake the whole course AND the test. Just like school. *As it is on earth, so shall it be in heaven.*

∞◊†∞◊†∞◊†∞◊†∞◊†∞

My mother said something that I mentioned earlier: MOVE OR BE MOVED! Our earthly parents are (or should be) an extension of our father in heaven. My mother demanding I do the work assigned to me is because she knows its importance. She saw the bigger picture. Now, I'm not religious, but I am a very spiritual person. The good thing about this is no matter your religion, creed, ethnic background or even sexual preference the same rules apply. *As it is with our earthly parents, so it is with our God.* The only difference with my mother is that I had a choice whether or not to obey. With God, I had a choice, but the outcome was already predestined. See the thing about being chosen is there's no way around it. You can't charm, talk or wiggle your way out of the calling that is placed on you. You will either MOVE OR BE MOVED!

What does that mean? It means that no matter how long or how far you try to run, no matter how much you fight; God will move you to where he needs you to be. He pursues the chosen. He prepares us by pushing us to our very maximum limit. And by pushing us to our limit, we are shown that we are limitless. He leads us to the water but, it is up to us to drink and see that it is good.

In the next few sections I will encourage you to M.O.V.E. yourself! I'd like to believe that if you are reading this book, you already know what it is you want to do. I even believe that you know how to physically go about it. I'm here to get you mentally and spiritually prepared for the calling God has placed on your life. Some are chosen to save lives; others are chosen to fix cars. It's not what you do, it's how you do it. I want to show you how to move with excellence. I'm going to help you find *"The Glow."*

∞◊†∞◊†∞◊†∞◊†∞◊†∞

Before we began, let me tell you about *"The Glow."* There was a movie I loved when I was young called *"The Last Dragon™."* Some of you may remember it. (If you get a chance and you can look pass the old-style cinematography of the movie you should check it out.) The movie focuses on "Bruce" Leroy Green, a kid from Harlem. Leroy loved martial arts and idolized Bruce Lee. In the beginning of the movie Leroy is training with his sensei. He looks to have mastered the art; fighting various obstacles around the room and catching an arrow out of the air...all with his eyes closed! To everyone else he looked to be a martial arts expert. His sensei told him otherwise. Leroy's teacher told that he would not reach the final level of The Dragon until he had *"The Glow."*

Leroy was good; great even. But what Leroy wasn't, was limitless. He still had doubts. When challenged by "Sho'Nuff, the shogun of Harlem," Leroy waivered in his confidence. He didn't have *"The Glow."* Sho'Nuff would kick Leroy's butt at every turn. He destroyed Leroy's family's business. He beat up his friends. He was so sure of himself that he had obtained *"The Glow"* long before Leroy even knew what it was. Leroy ran all around Harlem trying to find what it is that he needed to gain access to *"The Glow."*

People all over the city couldn't understand why he was looking for *"The Glow."* They told him that he was the Master, but Leroy didn't believe it. If you don't believe it you can't even begin to tap into the power that is within you. Why? If you believe something is not there you will never try to access it. It is not real to you.

Not until the end did Leroy reflect on the positive things he was told. He dwelled on those positive thoughts and in his final hour; Leroy obtained *"The Glow."* His glow was so great, so real that *"The Glow"* of Sho'Nuff began to fade. Leroy finally believed in himself. If not for Leroy's journey to find *"The Glow,"* he would have never learned the lessons necessary to succeed. To become limitless, Leroy had to M.O.V.E.

When you become limitless, when you believe in that power inside you; then you will achieve *"The Glow."* I'm sure you've heard the expression, 'my God, you're glowing!' That's because your inner joy and confidence is so real that it begins to shine from the inside out. People will begin to see things in you. They'll approach you and the right people will always seem to be in your path. That's *"The Glow."* Most people won't even know why they attract to you, but you will. And it all starts with belief. If you don't believe in yourself, if you don't believe in who you are and your capabilities, you will never be able to gain access to the unseen.

Each day you need to remind yourself of where you are headed. Similar to getting a song stuck in your head, singing the hook all day because you've heard it a million times. Eventually, you notice that you know the words without even trying. It's ingrained now. The same goes for you and your path to excellence. The more that you hear and talk to yourself about your dream, the more it gets ingrained into your mind and spirit. You must believe in it deeply, as if it's with you every day and you can touch it. Once you truly believe it, you'll be able to feel it.

Now, let's M.O.V.E!

CHAPTER ONE

M.O.V.E.

MAKE UP YOUR MIND

AND MOTIVATE YOURSELF

James 1:6-8

"...for he that wavereth is like a wave of the sea; driven with the wind and tossed. For let not that man think that he shall receive any thing of the Lord. A double minded man is unstable in all his ways."

I developed a saying after experiencing years of disbelief and procrastination. "The hardest part about doing it, is doing it." Think about that for a moment. The hardest part about doing anything is actually getting up to do it. There's a process internally before you make a move. That process starts with making up your mind. Before you get up off the couch to go grab that sandwich in the refrigerator, you have a thought. Before that thought, you identify a need within (your hunger). After identifying the need, you probably will consider what is in your fridge to eat or what may be in the pantry You may think:

> *There's a subway sandwich from earlier I stashed in the 'fridge. Hmmm... There's also that delicious spaghetti my wife made last night.*

You begin to think about things that can go with the spaghetti, your thoughts flourishing into a 3-course meal. With your meal set in your mind, you get up and get moving. You're hungry and nothing is going to stop you from feeding that hunger, right? Your mind is made up and it's time to execute your plan for spaghetti, garlic bread, and side salad, with a cold Pepsi to wash it all down!

Now, let's look at what may have happened if you were unsure. Let's say you just got up and went to the refrigerator with no idea what you wanted. You'd stand there with the refrigerator door open. The look of cold spaghetti deterring you from that 3-course meal. Not only did you waste time, you wasted energy; not only your physical energy but the energy from the light bulb shining in your refrigerator. Five or 10 minutes pass and you still haven't decided, so you shut the refrigerator door, convinced there's nothing to eat. Does this sound familiar?

That, my friend, is being double-minded. You don't know what you want. You haven't made your mind up that spaghetti is what you want, so you waver in your thinking when you are presented with other options like hot dogs or sub sandwiches. *Do I want spaghetti, or hot dogs, or maybe a sub?* Before you know it days, months, years have passed and you still haven't made up your mind. If you would just decide, your whole being will comply with that decision. Do you want spaghetti? Yes. Have you made up your mind? Yes. Well, now your mouth and stomach agree and prepare for the taste of spaghetti. You've heard it before. "*I got a taste for spaghetti!*" Whoever made that statement has gone through the necessary process to figure out what they want. I wonder, what do you have a taste for?

You must know that the prize is waiting for you just like the spaghetti in the refrigerator. But, instead of spaghetti you need to be hungry for success. It's not in your hands yet, but just like you know the spaghetti is in the refrigerator, you should know that success is just ahead.

You must find a way to believe in the intangible things in life. The intangible things are the most valuable. Things like faith, love, humility, and honor are the most prized possessions you can have. You can't see it or touch it, which means that once you obtain it, only you can lose it. Reach first for that which you cannot see.

First, make up your mind about what it is that you want to do. I don't care about what your mother wants you to do. Or what your teachers tell you. I don't care about the path your friends think you should take. What is it that will make YOU happy? What do YOU want to do? Make that decision first. This is one of those times where it's okay to be selfish. In the end, you are the one who must live with the decision.

∞◊†∞◊†∞◊†∞◊†∞◊†∞

How a hungry are you for success? Success to me is being happy. It's not about money or possessions. It's about how you feel about your life when you lay down at night. Only YOU can make YOU happy. Only you know what will make you happy. Sometimes what makes you happy will make others around you unhappy. I'm here to tell you that it's none of your business who's unhappy about what you are doing to make yourself satisfied with your life. If they are unhappy then your job is to make them as unhappy as possible. If you won't work for the happiness of yourself, if that's not enough motivation, then use your enemy as your leverage.

Someone told me "success is the best revenge." If someone tears you down with words; tells you that you can't achieve your destiny, your best weapon is silence and action. If you choose to dwell on the words of others, their beliefs will become your own. You will reap the consequences of someone else's thoughts of you and what you are doing.

Once you've made up your mind you must motivate yourself. You have to find something to keep you going after that goal. What's going to make you keep getting up after being knocked down? (And by the way, you WILL be knocked down.)

∞◊†∞◊†∞◊†∞◊†∞◊†∞

As I write this book, I am 35 and homeless in the Washington D.C. area. I'm not from here and have practically no one to lean on. I have a girlfriend here and sometimes a friend of hers may come around giving me food and money or even allowing me to escape the streets by letting me stay a night at her place. I have no family; none that I speak to anyway. My mother has dementia. My father gave up on me years ago (and I've JUST realized this recently). My siblings aren't around—they are busy living their own lives. I don't blame them for that. So, it's just me.

I spend more than 50% of my day alone. I've met other homeless people out here, but most of them have a negative outlook on life. They aren't aware of the power that awaits if they would just make up their minds to succeed. You become like those you surround yourself with if you aren't already like them. Who I keep in my company is just as important as maintaining a thought life that elevates me. No one will motivate and encourage me, but me. I'd walk to the corner of F and 13th daily with a sign that says:

> **HOMELESS:**
> Still Winning, but
> I NEED A JOB
> paying whatever an hour.

This is something I had never done before. I was trying to get something I never had. To motivate myself I would stand on this corner and deliver motivational speeches from the heart. I'd title my speeches things like "Greatness Undiscovered" and "Pushing through the Pain." I needed motivation. There was no one there to motivate me, but me. It was a matter of my dream living or dying. It wasn't enough for me to internally speak to myself. I had to hear what I was saying and I felt crazy walking around town speaking audibly to myself. So, I did something I'd never done before and it scared the sound out of me every time I stepped on that corner. Once I'd gotten past those first 5 minutes of speaking I went into auto pilot, speaking more boldly as time went by. I was motivating myself. Once I started to motivate myself other people would see my confidence and motivate me even more by saying "right" or "good stuff brother."

People would occasionally hear me from their car window at a stop light and offer me money. I never asked for their money. If it came it was a blessing, but I am able bodied and I feel to ask someone for their hard-earned money without earning it is immoral. I was focused on the result. I didn't care what people thought or how crazy I may have seemed. I HAD TO motivate myself and this was the most effective way.

It's easy to be deterred being homeless. The pressure of everyday life is enough to make anyone believe that their current situation is going to be their permanent situation. It doesn't have to be if you remain hard at work to change your situation.

Life's Law #6: "Hard work pays off." No person will work hard without reaping the benefits of their work. It just doesn't happen that way. Working hard means going at it every day for the reward of success. If you're not working hard with the intention of success, you may as well lock your car doors and leave the windows down. It's just senseless. What are you working for? If you're not working toward your own success then you are simply working to make someone else successful. Know your value. Do not allow anyone to put undue stress on you.

You know better than anyone your capabilities. If you work hard for yourself then it's you who reaps the benefits. Even if you are working for someone else, you should have an exit plan if you are planning to be your own boss. So even as you clock in and out on someone else's clock, the work you do is ultimately to benefit you. When you keep in mind what your goal is and who you are REALLY working for, it makes it easier to get up day to day and do it all over again.

∞◊†∞◊†∞◊†∞◊†∞◊†∞

There's a phrase we used in the streets when we would return to doing something we once put down. We would say "I'm back at it like a crack addict!" Some of you may know a crack addict. Others may have one in their family. Here's my point. A crack addict will do any kind of work, steal, lie, manipulate or whatever to get that drug. He doesn't care who gets in his way, who he hurts in the process, or who doesn't like it. He's addicted to the high and he has to have it. We all should be "at it like crack addicts." Every waking moment needs to be about your road to success. You should want it as bad as an addict wants to get high.

It should be daily, tireless, effort on your part to do whatever you can that day to make your dream come true. A crack addict isn't thinking about tomorrow, today. All an addict cares about is today. He's doing what needs to be done, today, to get what he wants...you guessed it, today! He has his mind made up every morning. As soon as he wakes, he begins working on the objective of the day. That objective is to get what he wants (it just so happens what he wants is terrible for his health). Say what you will, but there aren't many days that go by that a crack addict isn't successful in getting what he wants.

You must first make up your mind. Decide that you WILL be successful. Decide that you WILL go after the thing that God has placed in your heart and on your mind. Your mind must first be prepared for the task at hand. Make up your mind then motivate yourself to get up every day to go get it. Once your mind is made up to succeed your obstacles will no longer seem like they can't be conquered. You will no longer look at life's hardships like you used to, because your entire self is concentrated on the result. No one can stop a person whose mind is made up. You can slow them down, but you can't stop them. A person whose mind is made up will find a way to obtain whatever it is that they want. A person with a clear vision doesn't see failure as an option, no matter how often it may present itself.

CHAPTER TWO

M.O.V.E.

OBSERVE

AND

OVERCOME OBSTACLES

John 16:33

"These things I have spoken to you, so that in Me you may have peace. In the world you have tribulation, but take courage; I have overcome the world."

Let's start with that quote. This is Jesus speaking to his disciples. He says, "*these things I have spoken to you, so that in Me you may have peace.*" I believe that Jesus was saying, 'I've told you these stories so that you know that you too are capable of what I've done on this earth.' After all we are all made in God's image. Our spirits are directly connected to the Great Creator. He continues saying, "*In the world you have tribulation, but take courage; I have overcome the world.*" I believe Jesus encouraged his people by saying there will be tribulation in the world. He goes on to say don't worry about that, I have overcome the world. He was implying, in my opinion that we shouldn't worry about our day-to-day trials. He has overcome the world and we are just like him. What's a little storm here and there when the power to overcome the world is within us all?

We often get too excited when we have a new promising idea. We want to go out and get started right away. All we focus on is the result. No one really considers the hard road to glory. So, with bright eyes and bushy tails, we rush right into it with only an idea in place. An idea is just the destination. The plan is the vessel that gets you to that destination. Planning is the spine of your idea. It keeps things in correct order. Whatever that idea or vision is, you must observe every angle. Who's your competition? What is the correct market and demographic to promote your service or product?

Not only must you observe your organization's service or product, you should also observe yourself. Ask why you are doing this. Are you doing it for profit or passion? Are you doing it for both? What is the driving force that will keep you from quitting when obstacles present themselves? There has to be something more than money that drives you. You must have a passion for what you are doing. If you have no passion for what you are doing you will never make the necessary sacrifices to attain it.

There will be times where it will seem like this isn't your destiny. You may think to yourself, '*it shouldn't be this hard.*' But, yes it should be. You find your power in those times. If there is no passion to drive you, the chances of you quitting are much higher than they would be if you were reaching for something you TRULY want. There is no power in the weak. You will be tested. There will be obstacles. It takes mental and spiritual strength. To build strength you must push against resistance. It's just like working your physical body. The weight is the resistance. You have to lift that weight time and time again to build muscle. If you aren't working that muscle then it becomes weak. You become weak. But the more you work out, the more endurance you build.

The biggest obstacle is you. In fact, the *only* obstacle is you. Perception is everything. How you perceive a situation determines how you react. If you mind says you can't do it and you don't deal with those thoughts, they will become your reality. If you can get out of your own way, you can begin to experience your own true power. Confucius says: "*Weather you think you can or you think you can't, either way you're right.*" It's our own selves that get in our way. We see what is in front of us as permanent reality. I get it. It's hard to see past the pain. I know it's hard to see the glory at the end when you are stuck in the middle of storms. Those storms are necessary for you to fully enjoy your reward. If you give up, you'll never know what you can accomplish.

Everyone has a favorite celebrity. Most folks know everything about their person. You feel close with them through reading bios, magazine interviews, and watching them on T.V., doing what it is they do. You feel like you know this person. There is a story there; a story of pain and obstacles. Some are more painful than others. There isn't one person who got to their dream without some challenging work and pain.

I was motivated by pain. The more I would hurt the more I wanted to prove everyone wrong. I asked for pain. I would call my ex- girlfriends saying; 'go ahead, say what you feel. Don't hold back!" The pain was addictive. I hated it, but I loved it. I hated how it felt, but for some reason it's what I needed to move. I would have spurts of determination. I made the pain work. That's what I loved about it. At the same time, it could have been deadly. Some pain was unbearable at the time. Once I had my mind made up, the pain began to dull when it came about. I was too busy reaching for success to worry about what was going on outside it. I was being moved by my situations. I was being moved by the desire to no longer be homeless and hopeless.

One of the hardest things you will ever have to do is to work as if nothing bothers you. It's hard to continue when there is something eating at the very core of your being. Frankly, I don't know how I do it sometimes. All I know is that I've been through so much that pain isn't much of a thing to me anymore. It's so common in my life that some things just don't get my attention. I am so hell bent on getting to my glory that the pain is pushed to the back of my mind. Then I'm back thinking about what it is I can do daily, to get me a step closer to my destination in life.

I have one of the biggest obstacles to get over: Homelessness. This is an obstacle that I created. I put myself in this position. I have little to no resources. The computer I'm writing this book on isn't mine. I can only use the library's computer in 15-minute increments. I sometimes lose things I've already typed out. But I don't let my situation limit me anymore. I will not let my situation dictate how I choose to think. It doesn't define me. I do what I can. I write daily and I build relationships with a diverse crowd. I keep myself looking professional. I wear a shirt, tie, khakis and sneakers to deliver my motivational speeches street-side. I shave to make sure my hair isn't looking unkempt. I see myself as the person I want to be, not who I currently am. I didn't let the fact that I'm homeless limit me. When I introduce myself, telling people what I do, I say "I'm an author and motivational speaker." This will be what people see me as from then on. Why, because it's the first impression, and that's what sticks. It's just as effective as when you tell people your name for the first time. It sticks with most people. They will treat you according to what you say you are. That's more energy going toward the manifestation of who you aim to be. Now, people will inform you about things that coincide with what it is you said you do. If they come across work that requires a motivational speaker or an author they'll say, "oh, my new friend is an author!" Then they will pass on information, possible bookings, or whatever they've found that may be of assistance to you and your work.

I am who I say I am. Though I may not look like much it still doesn't make me who I am. My clothes, my appearance these things don't define who I am. A diamond is still a diamond even when it's in the mine. It doesn't start out shiny and polished like we see on the shelves of these jewelry stores. Someone saw the beauty in diamonds before the rest of the world did and made a killing. You must see the diamond in you. Just because the world hasn't recognized your greatness doesn't mean that it isn't there. It just hasn't been discovered by the world. You are the coal miner that sees the diamond in you. Believe in what you see.

Your obstacles are there for one thing, to prepare you. Failure doesn't mean you should quit. Failure is just an indication that your plan needs some extra attention or revision. You can't let it control your movements. Someone told me, 'we all go through s**t, just don't get stuck in it!" This means we should be always moving, even if it's just an inch at a time. There is still progress being made. Even as we are going through obstacles we are still moving. It may slow us down but, never stop us. We must keep running the race.

Even when you run you have to start slow. No one starts running at a full sprint. It isn't possible. There are levels to everything we do. We can't start at the top. We have to work our way to the top. The possibilities are limitless once you've mastered the pushing through the pain and overcoming obstacles. If you can overcome opposition and keep moving, success is yours.

CHAPTER THREE

M.O.V.E.

VERBALIZE

AND

VISUALIZE

Proverbs 18:21

"The tongue can bring death or life;

those who love to talk will reap the consequences."

(New Living Translation)

Let's discuss this scripture. It paints an accurate picture of the power of the tongue. There are people living, but are dead inside. They aren't alive, they're just living. Then there are those who are full of life and therefore, living life to its fullest. The things you say about yourself and the things you choose to believe that others may say about you can be a matter of life or death.

Earlier I spoke about getting a song stuck in your head and how the chorus seems to stain your memory after hearing it so much? Imagine that whatever you say about yourself and what others say about you becoming a part of your mental make-up. What we hear and what we continue to hear will become our belief. Our ears and eyes are a direct line to the brain. What we feed our brain will become second nature to us. What we say we are we will become. What we choose to believe we are we will become. You can choose to speak life or death into yourself. Parents, you can speak life or death into your children. What they see from you is what they will become. You are the first line of defense for your children and if you are calling him or her stupid, lazy, or anything negative, it will be what they believe. Your words are gospel to your children. What will you choose to say to them? There is life and death in the power of the tongue. Will you speak life or will you speak death into your child? Whatever you choose, you will reap the consequences of it.

Consequences don't have to be bad or negative. We often associate the word consequence with negativity. Consequence is defined as a result or effect of an action or condition. It doesn't matter if it's negative or positive the consequence is a result of an action or condition, which can be either positive or negative. It's all about the nature of the seed planted. If you plant negative words and thoughts the consequences are negative. If you plant positive the consequences are positive. Just like you can't get oranges from a lemon seed, you can't get positive results from negative output.

Some people like to use the term "tough love." To this day I have a tough time shedding that part of my personality. I'm a living testament that nothing positive comes out of tough love. Furthermore, love shouldn't be tough. There's nothing uplifting about talking down or negatively to a person so that they can use it for good. There's nothing enlightening about judging a person. It's not what you say, but how you say it. Tough love is just what it says, tough. There is no love in it if the person you are talking to doesn't leave the conversation feeling better about themselves or more conscious of their own flaws. Tough love doesn't promote change. It leaves most feeling beat down and upset. The words you use and the tone are negative in every way. Though it may not be the intention of the person who is talking, it still has a negative effect. Those words are still killing the person they're directed to.

∞◊†∞◊†∞◊†∞◊†∞◊†∞

In my youth, I aspired to become an entertainer. I didn't much care about what type of entertainment, I just wanted to be in the spotlight and show the world my talents. I used to rap, act, write poetry and stories, I even did stand-up comedy. One day as I was discussing my dreams with my mom and brother. I don't recall exactly what my mother said, but I will never forget the negativity I felt in that moment. After she said what she did, I responded asking, 'how could you just shoot my dreams down like that?" Everyone laughed. They thought my response was funny, but I was serious.

My mother never went to any of my shows. She never supported my dreams. She never spoke life into me. As a result, I grew up with low self-esteem. Her lack of support subconsciously made me believe that I was incapable of doing what I was meant to do. I remember two separate occasions where she allowed her tongue to speak death to me. My mistake was believing what she said about me. How could I not? This is my mom we're talking about. She is not supposed to steer me wrong, but she did.

It wasn't until I was well into my thirties before I started to believe otherwise. I can't account for my mother's mistakes. To fully blame her for the outcome of my life would mean I was giving her the power. Instead, I retain my power by taking responsibility for what I did wrong and learning from it. Though I knew nothing about the power I possessed in me to change my life, I still choose to let what was done and said to me control me.

I missed a lot of opportunities. Those words were a part of me. I accepted them as my truth. For years I held wasted talent because I didn't believe in myself. My parents were the first line of defense and although they didn't do a good job, I messed up by letting it drive my actions. It showed up in my life.

Parents, nurture the dreams of your children even if you don't understand them. They were born with a gift or a desire to do something. And what you say to them could be a matter of life and death. In return, you as a parent will also suffer consequences for the kind of life you built for your children. Will it be negative or positive? The choice is yours. I was a part of the walking dead for about 34 years of my life. I am now 37 and I have to reprogram my mentality on a regular basis because those words had lasting effects on me.

∞◊†∞◊†∞◊†∞◊†∞◊†∞

Muhammad Ali, Michael Jordan, and Jim Carrey are among an extensive list of celebrities who promote the power of visualization. All three have been very open about how the power of visualization has been a cornerstone in their personal success. Muhammad Ali was known for his visualization of each fight minute-by-minute. It has been proven by neuroscientists that the brain's activity is the same when visualizing as it is when it is happening. This means that our brain cannot between differentiate visualization and the actual act of doing something. It's quite amazing if you think about it. Visualization is the most powerful activity you can do when trying to reach a certain goal. The more details you imagine the stronger the outcome. We learn better from images. We can learn by auditory measures; it will find its way into our permanent memory, but visual images either with the eyes or in the brain; are committed to memory much quicker.

In a Catherine Chadwick article, she explains in detail how we should visualize to maximize the desired outcome while engaging in the activity itself. Here's how she explains it:

> *"In order to make visualization practice as beneficial as possible, it appears that honoring the neurology behind it is worth bearing in mind. This means getting to the point of being able to visualize oneself as if actually engaged in the desired activity in order to develop the neurological pathways. Breaking visualizations down into stages if necessary will ensure that the part of the brain that assists in planning a route to achievement will not be overwhelmed with too much data."*

When visualizing, don't place yourself in a scene from the outside looking in. You must imagine seeing from your eyes; your perspective. How does it feel? Where are you? Imagine as many details as you can, all the way down to the smell of your environment. Make it as real as possible. Remember to not overwhelm your brain with too much data. Place just enough detail in your vision to make it as real as possible. This is effective visualization. Allow yourself to feel all the feelings that come with what it is you are visualizing. The more you do it, the more real it becomes, until it is reality. "If you can conceive it you, can achieve it." This adage is also a law of life. If your mind can visualize and picture the desired outcome, then that outcome is attainable. The possibilities are never ending.

CHAPTER FOUR

M.O.V.E.

EXECUTE

AND

ELEVATE

"Without Strategy, execution is aimless.

Without execution, strategy is useless."

-Morris Chong CEO of TSMC

From this chapter's quote you can tell that strategy and execution are equally important in your journey to success. One cannot be without the other if you expect results. The execution of your plan is the last leg of whatever it is you are working toward. It's the final piece to the puzzle of success. Part of your strategy is trying to predict what could go wrong in the process. The point of execution says that you are ready to go get whatever it is that you are striving for. The plan has been put into order and the carrying out of these plans is now necessary. The hardest part is over. The part of doing is now in play.

What we must keep in mind is that there is no such thing as a flawless plan. Your plan can seem flawless but there is almost always some unforeseen glitch when it comes to the strategy. All of the information and knowledge gathered in your strategic planning should help you to avoid quitting. At this point, it wouldn't be smart to stop. You are right at the tipping point.

This reminds me of a picture I saw of two men working in a diamond mine. One man drilled closer to the diamonds. The other man was not too far behind, but he was behind. The guy who was closest to the diamonds quit with about a foot of digging left to do. The other man kept working without remorse. The first man never experienced success. He quit in his final hour. He didn't know it was his final hour. The only way he could have known was to continue executing his plan.

This isn't the time to give up. All the work is done. All that's left to do is to execute your plan. Execute your plan KNOWING it will work. If there's a bump in the road, some minor revision may be called for. Quitting should NOT be an option or even a thought. Concentrate on the complete execution of your plan. And do it with the thought of winning in mind. Do this, and I promise your time will come.

I've learned the amount of effort you put into anything is the amount of reward you will see. What do I mean by that? It's simple. If you spend 2 hours a week on your craft, you will get that much back from what you put in.

There's not much to be said about executing your plan. Most of the work is done if you've reached this point. The only thing to do now is work. Work your strategy to the end, and repeat the steps for your next venture. The more you do it, the easier it becomes. One venture will build a bridge for the next if done correctly. Changes in your mental process will begin to take place. After you've succeeded once, you will see the possibilities and your mind will begin to expect to be successful in whatever it conceives. The power in that change will excel your execution and your success. The possibilities are endless. If you think it's possible and you want it, that's when it's time to M.O.V.E.

Final Thoughts:

A Word from the Author

Whoever you are, wherever you are, I believe in you. I believe in your uncanny ability to mold your world into the perfect place for you. Unfortunately, it's not enough for me to believe in you. You must believe in you.

No matter your religion, color or creed success is available to you. It's is up to you to bring that picture in your mind to reality. It's not magic. It won't just appear out of nowhere. You must work hard to achieve it. Whatever you put your hands on will prosper if you follow these steps. Mixed with a little will and expectation you can begin to make positive things happen in your life.

Your inner-self, your spirit, your chi, your soul; whatever you choose to call the energy that is you, is made of the same things that created this world. You are an extension of the Great Creator. It doesn't matter what you call this entity. It speaks your language. Make known the desires of your heart. Don't ask, demand it; demand it from yourself. Let the true you shine without reservation. Don't be afraid to be different.

What is your perception of yourself? Who do you see when you look at you? You will become that which you believe you are. Is what you believe your own perception of you or is it what someone has told you over and over? Make up your mind and decide to work for you success. Once that takes place there's no one who can deter you from your path. It's your decision to decide what that path is and where it leads. Once you've come to that conclusion, you will be ready to M.O.V.E.

-B. A. Ross

Made in the USA
Middletown, DE
12 November 2020

23813892R00036